DISCOVER AMERICA

WYOMING

Janice Parker

www.av2books.com

MEDIA ENHANCED BOOKS

AV² BY WEIGL™

ADDED VALUE • AUDIO VISUAL

Go to **www.av2books.com**, and enter this book's unique code.

BOOK CODE

Z 3 4 8 4 3 2

AV² by Weigl brings you media enhanced books that support active learning.

AV² provides enriched content that supplements and complements this book. Weigl's AV² books strive to create inspired learning and engage young minds in a total learning experience.

Your AV² Media Enhanced books come alive with...

Audio
Listen to sections of the book read aloud.

Video
Watch informative video clips.

Embedded Weblinks
Gain additional information for research.

Try This!
Complete activities and hands-on experiments.

Key Words
Study vocabulary, and complete a matching word activity.

Quizzes
Test your knowledge.

Slide Show
View images and captions, and prepare a presentation.

... and much, much more!

Published by AV² by Weigl
350 5th Avenue, 59th Floor
New York, NY 10118
Website: www.av2books.com

Library of Congress Cataloging-in-Publication Data
Names: Parker, Janice, author.
Title: Wyoming : the Equality State / Janice Parker.
Description: New York, NY : AV2 by Weigl, 2016. | Series: Discover America |
   Includes index.
Identifiers: LCCN 2015047940 (print) | LCCN 2015048749 (ebook) | ISBN
   9781489649683 (hard cover : alk. paper) | ISBN 9781489649690 (soft cover :
   alk. paper) | ISBN 9781489649706 (Multi-User eBook)
Subjects: LCSH: Wyoming--Juvenile literature.
Classification: LCC F761.3 .P375 2016 (print) | LCC F761.3 (ebook) | DDC 978.7--dc 3
LC record available at http://lccn.loc.gov/2015047940

Printed in the United States of America, in Brainerd, Minnesota
1 2 3 4 5 6 7 8 9 20 19 18 17 16

082016
210716

Project Coordinator Heather Kissock
Art Director Terry Paulhus

Photo Credits
Every reasonable effort has been made to trace ownership and to obtain permission to reprint copyright material. The publisher would be pleased to have any errors or omissions brought to their attention so that they may be corrected in subsequent printings. The publisher acknowledges Getty Images, iStock Images, and Alamy as its primary image suppliers for this title.

WYOMING

Contents

STATE TREE
Plains Cottonwood

STATE BIRD
Meadowlark

STATE FLOWER
Indian Paintbrush

STATE FLAG
Wyoming

STATE MAMMAL
Bison

STATE SEAL
Wyoming

Nicknames
Equality State, Cowboy State, Big Wyoming

Motto
Equal Rights

Song
"Wyoming," words by C. E. Winter and music by G.E. Knapp

Population
(2010 Census) 563,626
Ranked 50th state

Entered the Union
July 10, 1890, as the 44th state

Capital
Cheyenne

Discover Wyoming

"Nature had collected all of her beauties together in one chosen place." Explorer John C. Frémont's description of Wyoming's landscape when he first set eyes on it in 1842 still rings true today. Since Frémont's time, many other visitors have admired the region's remarkable natural beauty, and many people have made the state their home.

Wyoming's natural attractions include Grand Teton National Park and Devils Tower. The 1,267-foot Devils Tower is a sacred site of worship for many Native Americans. According to legend, the marks on the side of the huge rock were made by the claws of a giant bear. Wyoming's inspirational landscape also has a special place in U.S. history. Most of Yellowstone National Park is located in the state, and Yellowstone was the first national park created by the U.S. government.

Much of Wyoming's terrain is rugged, which posed a challenge for the thousands of early pioneers who traveled through the region. For those pioneers who first settled in the area, a lack of good cropland made it difficult to earn a living. Today, Wyoming has a highly developed ranching tradition and is one of the country's most attractive recreational states. Its many lakes and rivers are used for boating and fishing. Forests full of plant and animal life attract hunters and wildlife observers. The mountains and parks are popular destinations for campers, hikers, and backpackers.

The Land

Grand Teton National Park includes some 310,000 acres and the Teton Range, a 40-mile-long mountain range. The first Europeans to travel in this area were fur trappers during the early to mid-1800s.

The name **Wyoming** is derived from a Native American word meaning "land of vast plains."

Wyoming's elevation is, on average, **6,700 feet** above sea level. This is the **second-highest** average in the nation, after **Colorado.**

Hundreds of thousands of pioneers followed the 2,200-mile Oregon Trail from the eastern United States to newly opened territory in the west.

Beginnings

The earliest visitors to Wyoming were prehistoric nomads who likely followed animal herds south from Alaska and Canada. Eventually, several cultures settled in Wyoming, and their descendants were those Native American groups present when European explorers came. The most prevalent group in the area was the Cheyenne.

The first Europeans to the Wyoming area arrived in the mid-eighteenth century. They were explorers and trappers. As the United States began expanding westward, small bands of settlers began following trappers out into Wyoming.

During Wyoming's pioneer days, the state was an essential corridor to the West. Most of the historic trails to the West cut through Wyoming. The Oregon, California, and **Mormon** trails brought settlers through the South Pass of the Continental Divide in west-central Wyoming. The Continental Divide is an imaginary line that runs from Alaska and Canada through the western states and the western side of South America. It is also known as the Great Divide.

The state's population grew steadily after the Union Pacific Railroad was built in the city of Cheyenne in 1867. The population was slow to grow and did not experience large booms, like in neighboring Colorado, because the state did not have large deposits of gold or silver. Instead, most settlers came for ranching and agriculture.

Where is WYOMING?

Wyoming is bordered by Montana to the north and northwest, South Dakota and Nebraska to the east, Colorado to the south, Utah to the southwest, and Idaho to the west. Getting around by land vehicle is relatively easy. Wyoming has an extensive network of state and federal roads. Interstate 25 runs north–south through the middle of the state. Interstate 80 runs east–west. Interstate 90 runs east–west in the northeast corner.

United States Map

Wyoming

Alaska   Hawai'i

MAP LEGEND

- ■ Wyoming
- ☆ Capital City
- ● Major City
- ◝ Bighorn National Forest
- ▲ Flaming Gorge
- ☐ Bordering States

IDAHO

UTAH

1 Cheyenne

Wyoming's capitol building in Cheyenne was built to resemble the U.S. Capitol in Washington, D.C. Its construction was authorized in 1886, and the cornerstone was laid the following year. Today, Cheyenne is steeped in the history of the Old West. Visitors can take trolley tours through the historic downtown.

2 Bighorn National Forest

Bighorn National Forest is the state's largest preserve of trees. Most of the tree species found in the state can be found within the protected forest. Bighorn also features an ancient Native American site called the Medicine Wheel. Many stones align into 28 spokes within the wheel and act as a calendar.

MONTANA

2

WYOMING

3

Laramie **3**

Cheyenne **1**

4

COLORADO

N

SCALE

0   50 miles

---

3 **Laramie**

Once known as a wild, lawless town in the west, Laramie is now a quiet college town. There are more than 20 locations listed on the National Registry for Historic Places in and around Laramie, preserving the area's rich history. Today, the city is a haven for outdoor enthusiasts.

4 **Flaming Gorge**

The hills and canyons of Flaming Gorge now rise from the pristine waters of Flaming Gorge Reservoir, created by damming the Green River. The Green River was the last unexplored river in North America. The Flaming Gorge recreation area features wide Wyoming landscapes where wild horses run.

Land Features

The easternmost third of the state is part of the Great Plains. This region's flat prairies and short grasses make it excellent for raising cattle and sheep. The rest of the state is covered by the Rocky Mountains. In this region, deep valleys and wide basins separate the mountain ranges.

About one-fifth of Wyoming is covered with forests. Trees such as pine, spruce, and fir are valuable natural resources. Most of the state's forests grow in the mountain regions, where rainfall is highest.

Devils Tower

In 1906, President Theodore Roosevelt declared Devils Tower the first U.S. national monument. He wanted to protect the landform and thought that Congress might take too long to make it a national park.

Teton Mountains

When land shifts around large cracks in Earth's crust, it is called faulting. The Teton Mountains are one of the best examples of block faulting. Stress inside Earth caused huge blocks of rock to lift. These landforms are called block mountains, or horsts.

Ayres Natural Bridge

Ayres Natural Bridge is one of the few natural bridges in the world to have water flowing under it.

Shoshone National Forest

Shoshone National Forest was the first national forest. It was designated a national forest in 1891 by President Benjamin Harris.

Climate

Temperatures can vary in Wyoming because of differences in elevation. The greatest amount of rain and snow falls in the mountains, while the plains receive little precipitation. In many areas, average high July temperatures range from 85° Fahrenheit to 95°F. In the mountains, the average July temperature is closer to 70°F. Wyoming's highest recorded temperature, 115°F, occurred in Basin on August 8, 1983. The lowest temperature, -66°F, was recorded at Riverside on February 9, 1933. Wyoming is one of the windiest states in the United States. Winds often reach 30 to 40 miles per hour (mph).

Average Annual Precipitation Across Wyoming

The average annual precipitation varies for different areas across Wyoming. How does location affect the amount of precipitation an area receives?

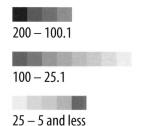

LEGEND

Average Annual Precipitation (in inches) 1961–1990

200 – 100.1

100 – 25.1

25 – 5 and less

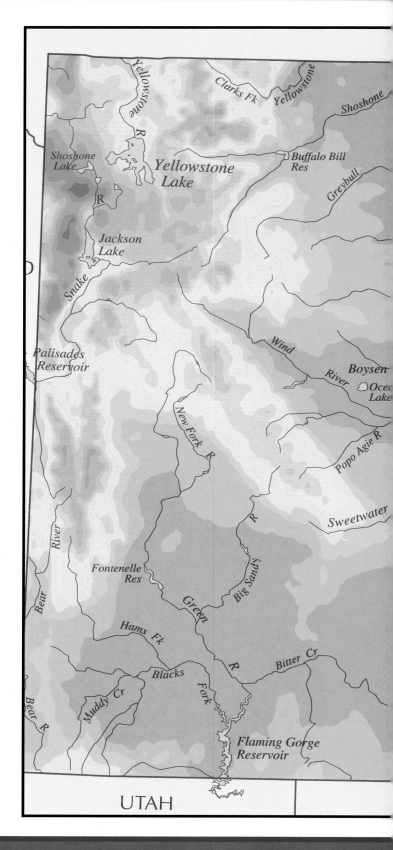

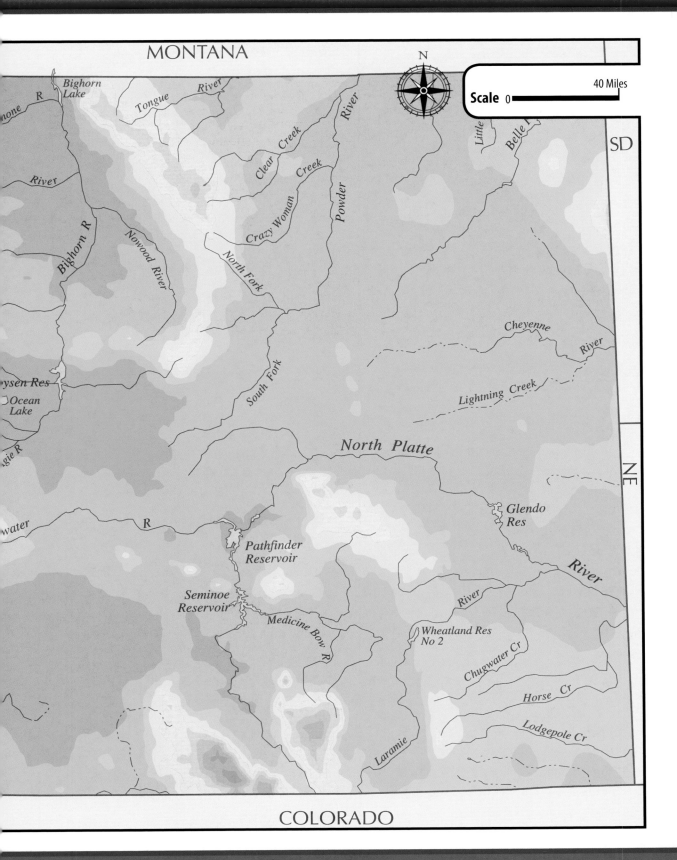

MONTANA

N

SD

Bighorn
Lake

Tongue   River

R

River

Clear Creek

Crazy Woman Creek

Powder   River

Little

Belle F

Nowood River

Bighorn R

North Fork

Crazy Woman

South Fork

Cheyenne

River

Lightning Creek

ysen Res

Ocean
Lake

gie R

North Platte

NE

water

R

Glendo
Res

Pathfinder
Reservoir

River

Seminoe
Reservoir

Medicine Bow

R

Wheatland Res
No 2

River

Chugwater Cr

Horse   Cr

Lodgepole Cr

Laramie

COLORADO

In 2010, Wyoming's logging industry harvested 33 million feet of timber.

Nature's Resources

Wyoming's lumber companies log Douglas firs, ponderosa pines, and lodgepole pines. Trees logged in Wyoming are used to make plywood, pulp, and paper products. This western state is rich in mineral resources. Wyoming is the nation's leader in trona mining. Trona is made up mostly of sodium carbonate. Chemicals made from trona are used to produce soap, baking soda, products used to purify water, and many other items. The state as a whole produces about 18 million tons of trona per year. Wyoming's trona industry employs about 3,000 people.

Wyoming's first wind farm was built in 1999 at Arlington, one of the state's windiest locations.

Large deposits of bentonite are also found in the state. Bentonite is an ingredient in glue, cosmetics, toothpaste, and paint. Other natural resources found in Wyoming include coal, natural gas, uranium, iron ore, limestone, and gypsum.

In the Powder River Basin, the coalfield produces more coal than any other field in the United States. Crude oil or natural gas is drilled in almost all of Wyoming's 23 counties. In a typical year, the state produces about 50 million barrels of crude oil, making it the seventh-largest oil-producing state. In 2014, Wyoming was the fifth largest producer of natural gas.

The wind is also a valuable natural resource. The U.S. Energy Information Administration has called southern Wyoming one of the best places in the nation for generating electricity using wind power. Gusts of wind often register at 50 to 60 mph.

Wyoming is one of the nation's leading producers of coal.

Most of the oil and natural gas deposits in the state are centered around the northeastern regions.

Vegetation

Trees of many kinds grow in the mountains and along the streams of Wyoming. Most are conifers, which are cone-producing trees. The lodgepole pine grows well in the higher mountains of Wyoming, where the climate is cool and wet. Douglas fir trees are plentiful, and aspens, cottonwoods, and willows are also common.

About four-fifths of the land is covered with grasses and the types of shrubs that survive in desert or desertlike conditions. Mosses, **lichens**, and wildflowers, such as Indian paintbrush and forget-me-nots, are also found in Wyoming. Sagebrush and western wheatgrass flourish in the lowlands. The driest regions of the state are home to plants that require little water to grow, such as yuccas and cacti.

Indian Paintbrush

The Indian paintbrush is Wyoming's state flower. It is also known as the painted cup.

Glacier Lily

Glacier lilies are bright spring flowers found at elevations above 7,500 feet.

Lodgepole Pine

Lodgepole pines are mainly found in the south-central area of the state.

Sagebrush

Sagebrush is the main vegetation found in the Wyoming Basin Shrub Steppe, an area drained by the Green, Wind, Bighorn, and North Platte Rivers.

Wildlife

Wyoming has more pronghorns than anyplace else in the world. Pronghorns are more numerous than people in Wyoming. The state also has the world's largest elk herd. Deer are found throughout the state, moose wander the northwestern region, and herds of bison, or buffalo, roam Yellowstone and Grand Teton national parks. Bighorn sheep live in the northern part of the state. Wyoming also has rabbits, coyotes, and bobcats living within its borders.

Many birds make their home in Wyoming. The sage grouse lives throughout the state. Other birds in Wyoming include pheasants, partridges, wild turkeys, white pelicans, trumpeter swans, and whistler swans. Bass, walleye, perch, channel catfish, trout, and many other species of fish swim in Wyoming's rivers and lakes.

Pronghorn

Pronghorns can run at speeds of about 60 miles per hour. Nearly half of all pronghorns in North America are found in Wyoming.

Horned Toad

The state reptile is the horned toad. The "toad" is actually a lizard.

Sage Grouse

Adult sage grouse are the largest of North American grouse species. The sage grouse was recently put under state protection to increase its numbers.

Elk

Elk from the National Elk Refuge at Jackson Hole are sent to other parts of the country to help other herds grow bigger and stronger.

Economy

Old Faithful

Old Faithful expels between 3,700 and 8,400 gallons of hot water per eruption.

Tourism

Yellowstone National Park is Wyoming's most popular tourist destination. The park, which extends into Montana and Idaho, is known for its geysers, which are hot springs that shoot jets of hot water and steam into the air. The best-known geyser in Yellowstone is Old Faithful, whose blasts can last for up to five minutes and can reach more than 170 feet in height.

Grand Teton National Park rivals Yellowstone as the most picturesque park in Wyoming. Located in northwestern Wyoming, Grand Teton National Park features some of the youngest mountains in the Rockies. The park has more than 200 miles of trails.

Dude Ranches

Dude ranches are resorts that offer visitors a variety of ranching experiences. Most of these vacation destinations offer a personal horse for the time of a visitor's stay.

Fort Laramie

Fort Laramie National Historic Site is another popular destination in Wyoming. Significant people in the history of the Old West who passed through the fort include Kit Carson, Crazy Horse, and Wyatt Earp.

Wyoming Dinosaur Center

Visitors to the Wyoming Dinosaur Center in Thermopolis can tour the museum or participate in an archaeological dig. The museum has dozens of full-size skeletons.

After petroleum and natural gas, coal is the most important fuel source mined in Wyoming.

Primary Industries

Mining is Wyoming's most important industry. The state produces about 40 percent of the nation's coal. A portion of the state's coal is burned to create electricity, which is used in Wyoming and also sold to other states.

The recession in 2009 and 2010 greatly affected the United States. Wyoming's natural gas and oil production protected the state during this time. Manufacturing plants utilize the raw materials mined in the state. The refining of petroleum and the processing of coal are especially important. Wyoming's chemical plants produce fertilizers and other agricultural chemicals.

Another major industry is tourism. Overall, the state's service industries, including tourism, provide many of the jobs in the state. In service industries, workers help or provide a service for other people. People who work in banks, hospitals, stores, and restaurants are all service workers.

It is estimated that Wyoming is sitting on about **one-third of the total uranium reserves** in the entire U.S.

The **service sector** employs about half of Wyoming's workers. Of these, many work in Wyoming's numerous state parks and forests.

Value of Goods and Services (in Millions of Dollars)

The mining of fuels such as coal, oil, and natural gas accounts for a significant amount of the state's economy. These fuels are nonrenewable. Once they have been used, they are gone. How might Wyoming make the best use of these resources and protect its economy over time?

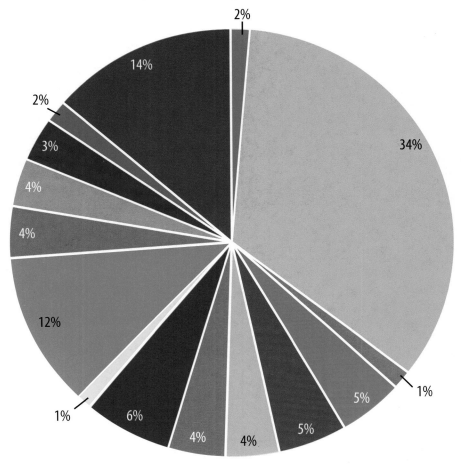

● Agriculture, Forestry, and Fishing	$710	○ Information	$585
○ Mining	$14,906	● Finance, Insurance, and Real Estate	$5,114
● Utilities	$651	● Professional and Business Services	$1,637
● Construction	$2,067	● Education, Health and Social Services	$1,622
● Manufacturing	$2,179	● Recreation and Accommodations	$1,458
○ Wholesale Trade	$1,679	● Other Services	$661
● Retail Trade	$1,868	● Government	$5,945
● Transportation and Warehousing	$2,719		

Cattle accounts for two-thirds of Wyoming's agricultural economy.

Goods and Services

Almost all of the agricultural land in Wyoming is used for ranching. Cattle and sheep are important to the state's economy. The sheep are raised mainly for wool, and Wyoming is a national leader in wool production.

Wyoming has little cropland because there is not enough precipitation to grow most crops. Farms that are **irrigated** can grow beans, potatoes, corn, and sugar beets. Some land is dry-farmed for crops such as barley, wheat, and hay. Rather than relying on irrigation, this type of farming usually involves plowing deep into the earth and planting seed in the fall, when it is cooler.

Various types of machinery, such as construction and farm equipment, are produced in Wyoming's factories. Food processing plants produce dairy and bakery items. Wyoming also manufactures stone, clay, and glass products.

About one-half of Wyoming's workers are employed in the service sector. A large percentage of service workers are employed by the federal government, the state government, or local governments. Some of these people work in the national forests and parks. Others work at the Francis E. Warren Air Force Base near Cheyenne.

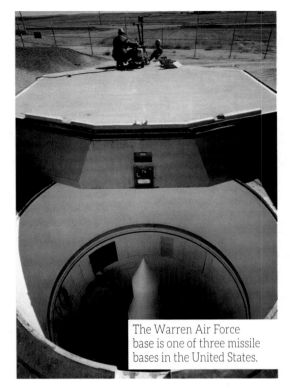

The Warren Air Force base is one of three missile bases in the United States.

Much of Wyoming's manufacturing industry is based on turning raw materials produced in the state into manufactured products. This includes oil refineries, which turn crude oil into fuel that can run cars and homes.

Perhaps one of the most well-known Shoshone in U.S. history is Sacajawea. She and her husband joined explorers Meriwether Lewis and William Clark in late 1804. Sacajawea acted as an interpreter between the expedition and various Native American groups.

The Shoshone name came from their word for long grass, *sosoni*. Some neighboring groups called them Shoshone, meaning Grass House People, based on the homes they sometimes made from the tall grasses of the plains.

Native Americans

It is believed that people were living in what is now Wyoming at least 12,000 years ago. These early residents lived in caves and hunted big game, such as **mammoths** and bison. Some of these groups left behind pictures that were carved and painted onto rocks.

Over time, many Native American groups settled in Wyoming. One of the largest was the Shoshone. Other Native American communities included the Arapaho, Crow, Cheyenne, Blackfoot, Ute, and Bannock. Most of the groups were nomadic, moving frequently to hunt animals, especially bison.

When European explorers first began to visit the area, Wyoming's population was probably less than 10,000. The explorers were followed by fur trappers and traders. The lives of the Native Americans in the area changed drastically in the 1800s as growing numbers of settlers of European descent arrived.

At first, relations between the Native Americans and the settlers were peaceful, and the groups traded with each other. However, Native Americans began to die from smallpox and other diseases carried by the new arrivals. In addition, the settlers took over or destroyed much of the Native American hunting grounds. Bitter fighting erupted over control of the land. By the late 1800s, most of the Native Americans had been driven out of the region.

Exploring the Land

It is believed that the first Europeans to explore what is now Wyoming were the French Canadian brothers François and Louis Joseph de La Vérendrye. They visited the area in 1743 while unsuccessfully searching for a route to the Pacific Ocean. In the early 1800s, John Colter entered the region. He had been an explorer, but changed focus and became a fur trapper and trader.

Timeline of Settlement

1812 Robert Stuart builds the first known cabin in the region, on the North Platte River near Bessemer Bend.

1825 The time in the fur trade known as the **rendezvous** period begins. The majority of Wyoming trappers work for fur companies, which ship most of the furs to Europe. "Free trappers" trade bear and other furs to the highest bidder.

1807 John Colter is the first explorer to see and describe the geysers at Yellowstone.

First Settlements

1834 Fort Laramie is established as the first permanent trading post.

1743 Brothers François and Louis Joseph de La Vérendrye reach what is now Wyoming. They are the first Europeans to travel this far northwest.

1842 Captain John C. Frémont makes his first expedition to Wyoming.

Early Explorers and Traders

In the early 1800s, hundreds of men traveled to Wyoming to work as trappers and to trade with the Native Americans for valuable furs. These trappers, called mountain men, assembled each year at a gathering called a rendezvous. They traded with Native Americans, held great feasts, played games, sang songs, and danced. Eventually, forts were built, and they became the meeting places. A typical early rendezvous lasted a couple of days, while later ones were often several months long.

The Green River Rendezvous was an important annual meeting of Wyoming's trappers, traders, and Native Americans. The last rendezvous was held in 1840. By that time, so many beavers had been hunted for their fur that the beaver population in the region had greatly declined.

1886 The Northwestern Railroad reaches the eastern edge of Wyoming. The Cheyenne and Northern Railway reaches Douglas.

1868 The Wyoming Territory is established. The next year, the first governor, John A. Campbell, takes office.

1889 The Wyoming Constitutional Convention is held.

Territory and Statehood

1852 The first school for children opens at Fort Laramie.

1890 In July, President Benjamin Harrison signs the act that admits Wyoming to the Union as the 44th state.

1843 Fort Bridger, the second permanent settlement, is established.

Historians estimate that 55,000 people traveled west on the Oregon Trail in 1850.

The First Settlers

Many settlers traveled through Wyoming on the Oregon Trail. Fort Laramie was the last major place to rest and purchase supplies before entering the mountains. Once through the mountains, the settlers reached Independence Rock, where they carved their names and messages into the stone. This was their way of letting friends and family who followed know that they had made it through the mountains safely.

Some of the people who entered Wyoming decided to settle in the area. The settlers often killed or drove away animals that the Native Americans depended on for food. There were many battles during the early years of settlement over land rights and hunting grounds. In 1851, Native Americans in Wyoming began signing a series of peace **treaties** with the U.S. government. According to the treaties, the Native Americans would allow forts, roads, and railroads to be built in exchange for land.

In 1867, the first train of the Union Pacific Railroad reached Cheyenne. Cities sprang up along the new railroad lines, and people came to work on the railroads. Others arrived to purchase cheap land or to open businesses.

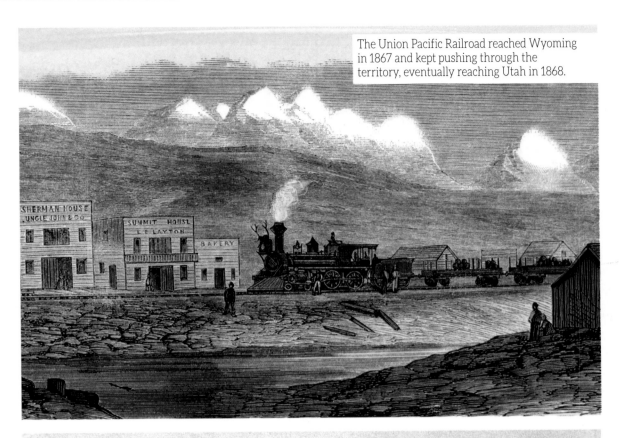

The Union Pacific Railroad reached Wyoming in 1867 and kept pushing through the territory, eventually reaching Utah in 1868.

Although Native American groups signed treaties with the United States for land, settlers continued pouring into the area, pushing Native American groups farther and farther west.

History Makers

Wyoming has had its share of people who made exceptional contributions to their state and nation. Notable Wyomingites have played key roles in the settlement of the western United States. Others have served in important government positions, have broken down gender barriers, and become leaders in their fields.

Francis E. Warren (1844–1929)

Francis Warren received the Congressional Medal of Honor for his bravery in the Civil War. He moved to Wyoming in 1868, where he pursued interests in ranching and real estate. In the years that followed, he served in a variety of public capacities for the territory and then the state.

Joseph M. Carey (1845–1924)

Joseph M. Carey campaigned for presidential candidate Ulysses S. Grant. During Grant's presidency, he was appointed U.S. district attorney for Wyoming. It was Carey who wrote the bill that admitted Wyoming to statehood. After Wyoming became a state, he was a U.S. senator and a state governor.

William F. Cody (1846–1917)

William Frederick Cody delivered mail for the **Pony Express**. After Civil War service, he was a U.S. Army scout. He hunted buffalo to feed railway crews, attaining celebrity status as "Buffalo Bill." Newspapers featured his dramatic fights with Native Americans, and he used his fame to start a traveling show about the Wild West. One of his homes was in Cody.

Nellie Taylor Ross (1876–1977)

During the 1924 election for governor, Nellie Taylor Ross defeated her rival by more than 8,000 votes to become the first female governor of any U.S. state. In 1933, President Franklin Roosevelt named her the director of the U.S. Mint, another first for a woman.

Anne Gorsuch Burford (1942–2004)

Anne Gorsuch Burford was born in Casper. She was appointed the administrator of the Environmental Protection Agency when Ronald Reagan was president. Burford, a Conservative, served in the Colorado House of Representatives before going to Washington, D.C.

Culture

There are no significant urban areas in Wyoming. Most of the state's residents live in rural communities.

While Wyoming's Native American population is small, they work hard to keep their culture and traditions alive.

The People Today

Wyoming has the smallest population of all the 50 states. In the 2010 Census, 563,626 people called the Equality State home. Cheyenne is the largest city, with a population of about 57,000. Casper follows closely behind, with a population of about 55,000. Other major cities are Laramie, Gillette, Rock Springs, and Sheridan. Cities and towns play an important role in Wyoming. With so few people and so much land, towns are a place for people to meet and stay in touch with their distant neighbors.

About nine-tenths of Wyoming's population is of European descent. The largest minority in Wyoming are Hispanic Americans. Wyoming has a very small Asian and African American population, and they mostly live in the urban areas of Cheyenne. About two percent of the population are Native Americans, mostly Arapaho and Shoshone. More than half live on the large Wind River Reservation.

Wyoming's population **grew** by more than 14 percent from **2000 to 2010**, almost one and a half times the national average.

Q What are some reasons for the recent dramatic population growth in the state?

The Wyoming state capitol was built between 1886 and 1890.

State Government

Wyoming's state government is divided into three branches. As in other states, these are the legislative, the executive, and the judicial branches. The legislative branch creates laws for the state and consists of a House of Representatives and a Senate. There are 30 state senators elected to four-year terms and 60 representatives elected to two-year terms. The executive branch of government enforces state laws. It is headed by the governor. The judicial branch is made up of the state's courts. The Supreme Court, the state's highest court, has five justices who serve eight-year terms.

Wyoming is divided into 23 counties. Each county is governed by a board of commissioners. The commissioners are elected to four-year terms.

The Wyoming state capitol building, which hosts both houses of the state government, was added to the National Register of Historic Places in 1973 and named a National Historic Landmark in 1987.

Before becoming Wyoming's governor in 2011, Matt Mead served as an attorney and was appointed the United States Attorney for the District of Wyoming in 2001.

Wyoming's state song is
"On, Wyoming!"

*In the far and mighty West,
Where the crimson sun seeks rest,
There's a growing splendid
State that lies above,
On the breast of this great land;
Where the massive Rockies stand,
There's Wyoming young and strong,
the State I love!
Wyoming, Wyoming!
Land of the sunlight clear!
Wyoming, Wyoming!
Land that we hold so dear!
Wyoming, Wyoming!
Precious art thou and thine!
Wyoming, Wyoming!
Beloved State of mine!*

* excerpted

The Eastern Shoshone Indian Days is an annual event that celebrates traditional culture, art, and dance.

Celebrating Culture

Wyoming's Native Americans have a rich cultural **heritage**. Every year they hold powwows to celebrate their history and traditions. Powwows were traditionally held to celebrate such events as major hunts and marriage ceremonies. Today, they can range from family reunions to major cultural events that attract Native Americans from all over the country.

The Shoshone and Arapaho hold many powwows during the summer on the Wind River Indian Reservation. Dancing competitions are popular events at these powwows. Visitors to these celebrations can also experience traditional Native American arts, crafts, and foods. In addition, the reservation has several cultural centers that allow visitors to learn more about Native American customs and history.

Cowboys have played an important role in Wyoming's history, and cowboy culture has remained an important aspect of Wyoming life. Many communities celebrate the state's ranching heritage with rodeos. Cowboy ballads are the official folk music of Wyoming. Many of the original ballads came from the cowboys who took part in the cattle drives of the late 1800s. Today, traditional cowboy music is still sung on the range and can be heard at county fairs and other state celebrations. Cowboy poetry contests and readings are another celebration of cowboy tradition.

The Carbon County, Wyoming, hosts the annual Grand Encampment Poetry Gathering. Each July, cowboy poets come together to give readings, enjoy cook-offs, and sign books.

Wyoming celebrates its pioneer heritage in parades and festivals throughout the state, including the annual Frontier Days celebration.

Singers, bands, and festivals throughout the state, such as the Jackson Hole Old West Days, pay homage to cowboy and country music.

Arts and Entertainment

Festivals and other cultural events define the seasons in Wyoming. The town of Douglas hosts the popular Wyoming State Fair each summer. In addition to typical rodeo events, the fair features a demolition derby and pig-wrestling contests. Sheridan hosts the Big Horn Mountain Festival, featuring **acoustic**, folk, bluegrass, and other traditional music.

The University of Wyoming has classical music groups, including a symphony orchestra and a choir. The Grand Teton Music Festival, held annually in Jackson Hole, typically features some 40 concerts. Every Fourth of July, Jackson Hole holds a free outdoor concert as part of the festival. The concert attracts thousands of people. Also associated with the event is the Festival Orchestra, an ensemble featuring some of the country's leading classical musicians.

Bill Nye, later famous for his TV show *Bill Nye the Science Guy*, started his career in Wyoming by editing the *Laramie Boomerang* newspaper.

NEWS

Artist **Jackson Pollock**, known for his abstract paintings, was born in Cody, Wyoming.

Museums offer year-round entertainment. The National Museum of Wildlife Art in Jackson Hole contains about 5,000 works of art in its collection, many of which were inspired by Wyoming. Buffalo Bill Cody founded the town of Cody. The town's Buffalo Bill Center of the West features a gallery of Western art, several museums, and a research library. A museum dedicated to Buffalo Bill has cowboy gear, firearms, and other artifacts from his life.

The Frontier Days Old West Museum boasts exhibits featuring artifacts from all facets of Wyoming's early history.

The Buffalo Bill Center of the West is divided into five museums that exhibit not only artifacts from Bill Cody's life, but also local history and Native American life.

Sports and Recreation

Wyoming is known for many sports, including rock-climbing and ballooning, but it is best known for rodeo sports. Rodeo events are considered some of the most dangerous in the world. Popular events include saddle **bronco** riding, bareback bronco riding, bull riding, steer wrestling, and calf roping. In bull riding, contestants try to remain on a bucking bull. In steer wrestling, or bulldogging, competitors jump from their horse onto a steer, grab it by the horns, and then pin it to the ground. During calf-roping and steer-roping contests, participants race to see how quickly and how well they can capture and tie up the animals.

Wyoming hosts the **world's largest rodeo**. It is held during Cheyenne's annual Frontier Days celebrations.

The University of Wyoming's **1943** star basketball player, **Kenny Sailor**, is believed to have invented the **jump shot**.

Wyoming's Frontier Days is an annual celebration of cowboy life. It has been held each year since 1897.

Both Yellowstone National Park and Grand Teton National Park provide many opportunities for outdoor recreation. Hiking, camping, and nature walks are popular in the forests and mountains of Yellowstone. Grand Teton is an ideal location for backpacking, climbing, canoeing, and fishing.

Hunting is yet another popular sport in Wyoming. Men and women can apply for licenses to hunt elk, deer, antelope, moose, bighorn sheep, and other animals. Fishing is also a favorite in the state's 15,846 miles of fishing streams and 297,633 acres of fishing lakes.

In the winter months, skiing and snowshoeing are common activities in Grand Teton National Park. Wyoming has a number of popular ski resorts. Snowmobiling and sled-dog racing are also popular winter pursuits.

Wyoming's high, snowy mountains provide excellent ski slopes.

Grand Teton National Park provides not only scenic hiking opportunities, but also adventurous mountain climbing.

Get To Know
WYOMING

Wyoming was the first state to construct a ranger station for its parks and forests. The station was built in 1891.

THE TOWN OF CODY CALLS ITSELF THE RODEO CAPITAL OF THE WORLD. IT HOLDS A RODEO EVERY NIGHT DURING THE SUMMER.

YELLOWSTONE NATIONAL PARK CONTAINS THE GREATEST CONCENTRATION OF GEYSERS IN THE WORLD.

WYOMING'S STATE DINOSAUR IS THE **TRICERATOPS**. THE STATE IS ONLY ONE OF SIX IN THE U.S. TO HAVE AN OFFICIAL DINOSAUR.

Wyoming is nicknamed the **Equality State** because its constitution was the first in the world to grant women the right to vote and hold office.

The term ¨dude ranch¨ was started in Wyoming.

It is estimated that about **400,000** pioneers passed through Wyoming between 1841 and 1868 on their way out west.

Brain Teasers

What have you learned about Wyoming after reading this book? Test your knowledge by answering these questions. All of the information can be found in the text you just read. The answers are provided below for easy reference.

1 What is the capital of Wyoming?

2 Why was Wyoming an essential corridor to the West for pioneers?

3 Where is Wyoming's largest preserve of trees?

4 Where in Wyoming does the most rain fall?

5 What was the United States' first National Park?

6 Which was the largest Native American group to settle in Wyoming?

7 Who was the first explorer to see and describe the geysers at Yellowstone?

8 When did the first Union Pacific Railroad train reach Cheyenne?

ANSWER KEY
1. Cheyenne 2. Could catch the Oregon, California, or Mormon Trail 3. Bighorn National Forest 4. Mountains 5. Yellowstone 6. Shoshone 7. John Colter 8. 1867

Key Words

acoustic: of or relating to a musical instrument that is not electric

bronco: a rodeo horse that tries to buck off a rider

heritage: traditions that result from a person's natural situation

irrigated: watered by artificial means

lichens: crusty growth found on rocks or tree trunks which results from fungus growing with algae

mammoths: prehistoric fur-covered elephant-like animals

Mormon: of or relating to the Church of Jesus Christ of Latter-day Saints

Pony Express: an early system for transporting mail using horses and riders

rendezvous: French for "a meeting"

treaties: formal agreements between two governments

Index

Log on to www.av2books.com

AV² by Weigl brings you media enhanced books that support active learning. Go to www.av2books.com, and enter the special code found on page 2 of this book. You will gain access to enriched and enhanced content that supplements and complements this book. Content includes video, audio, weblinks, quizzes, a slide show, and activities.

AV² Online Navigation

Audio
Listen to sections of the book read aloud.

Book Pages
AV² pages directly correspond to pages in the book.

Video
Watch informative video clips.

Key Words
Study vocabulary, and complete a matching word activity.

Embedded Weblinks
Gain additional information for research.

Quizzes
Test your knowledge.

Slide Show
View images and captions, and prepare a presentation.

Try This!
Complete activities and hands-on experiments.

AV² was built to bridge the gap between print and digital. We encourage you to tell us what you like and what you want to see in the future.

Sign up to be an AV² Ambassador at www.av2books.com/ambassador.

Due to the dynamic nature of the Internet, some of the URLs and activities provided as part of AV² by Weigl may have changed or ceased to exist. AV² by Weigl accepts no responsibility for any such changes. All media enhanced books are regularly monitored to update addresses and sites in a timely manner. Contact AV² by Weigl at 1-866-649-3445 or av2books@weigl.com with any questions, comments, or feedback.